BRITAIN IN OLD PHOTOGRAPHS

STOKE NEWINGTON, STAMFORD HILL & UPPER CLAPTON

D0294042

A family leaves Clissold House after taking refreshments and heads towards the children's playground in the summer of 1927. The spire of the new St Mary's Church rises in the background.

BRITAIN IN OLD PHOTOGRAPHS

STOKE NEWINGTON, STAMFORD HILL & UPPER CLAPTON

DAVID MANDER & BILL MANLEY

LONDON BOROUGH OF HACKNEY

ALAN SUTTON PUBLISHING LIMITED

Alan Sutton Publishing Limited
Phoenix Mill · Far Thrupp · Stroud
Gloucestershire · GL5 2BU

First published 1995

Copyright © text David Mander & Bill Manley
© photographs Dick Whetstone, except pp. 10,
14 bottom, 15 top, 21 bottom, 34 top, 38–41,
43 top, 44 bottom, 52 bottom, 63 bottom,
64, 65, 76 top, 78, 155 (all London Borough of
Hackney, Hackney Archives Department).

*Cover photograph: (front) Clissold House and
the spire of St Mary's Church, 1927; (back)
Stoke Newington fire brigade, c. 1905.*

British Library Cataloguing in Publication Data.
A catalogue record for this book is available from
the British Library.

ISBN 0-7509-1072-0

Typeset in 9/10 Sabon.
Typesetting and origination by
Alan Sutton Publishing Limited.
Printed in Great Britain by
Hartnolls, Bodmin, Cornwall.

Bill Manley (1928–93)

Bill Manley was born on 24 November 1928 at University College Hospital. His family lived in Islington until 1936, when they moved to Stoke Newington. A civil servant in his working life, latterly in the Ministry of Defence, he was keenly interested in the theatre and appeared in a Stoke Newington Labour League of Youth production which was the borough's contribution to the 1951 Festival of Britain. In 1954 he joined the Tower Theatre, which had opened a year before, beginning as a set painter and then moving on to lighting, sound and stage management. He appeared in pantomime in the mid-1950s, graduating from the back end of a horse to the front end of a lion, and he accompanied the Tower company to Edinburgh in 1961, playing various parts. Back in Islington in the 1970s he appeared in *The Recruiting Officer*, *Measure for Measure*, *Macbeth* and *A Penny for a Song*. When the Tower began its old time music hall in the 1960s, its productions owed much to Bill's researches, and he became the theatre's musicologist, drawing on his knowledge and song-sheet collection. He assisted with the production of a cassette of First World War songs, *Great Songs of the Great War*, and can be heard on it, performing under his uncle's name, Bill Bradley.

Bill was a member of many societies, including the Society for Theatre Research, the British Music Hall Society, the Ephemera Society, the English Folk Song and Dance Society, the Islington Society and the Friends of Hackney Archives, contributing articles and advice. His bushy, bearded figure was a familiar sight in the Marquis Tavern, Canonbury, and in the bar of the Tower Theatre, in either of which he could be sighted with a pint pot in one hand and frequently with a banana sticking out of his top pocket. His inevitable greeting was 'Mornin', whatever the time of day. One record office he frequented knew him as 'The Man of Mystery', as he was always very close with his address and insisted that all mail be forwarded via the Tower Theatre. His published works included an article on the Gainsborough Film Studios in 1986 for the *Hackney Terrier* (the newsletter of the Friends of Hackney Archives), a contribution to *The Illustrated Victorian Songbook* by Aline Waites and Robin Hunter (1984) and *Islington Entertained* (1990) on the local music halls and theatres. Bill also took an active part in the preservation of theatres and their archives, and was specially pleased when Hackney Archives Department managed to purchase a fine collection of early and mid-nineteenth-century theatre playbills from the Grecian and Eagle Theatre, celebrated in the rhyme 'Pop Goes the Weasel'. Bill Manley died suddenly on 30 January 1993.

David Mander
(with thanks to *Noises Off*, the newsletter of
the Tower Theatre, for material in compiling
this brief biographical note)

Contents

When Stoke Newington became a borough in 1900 it created its own coat of arms (left), incorporating the old St Mary's Parish Church, a tree representing the woodlands that once covered much of the parish, the silver sword of St Paul (representing the manorial control once exercised by the clergy of St Paul's Cathedral), and the scimitars from the County of Middlesex, upside down! This initial effort was replaced by a version authorized by the College of Arms in 1934. Hackney's arms (right) were approved from the start and needed no later revision.

C.J. and A. Algar ran a wholesale and retail stationers at No. 180 Stoke Newington Road from the end of the nineteenth century until shortly before the First World War. Books and magazines formed part of their stock and they also published their own postcards, though the work seems to have been undertaken by the specialist card producer, Charles Martin, who had his printing done in Berlin. This perfect moment dates from 1907.

Introduction

Welcome to the third selection of old photographs of the London Borough of Hackney, this time drawing on the extensive postcard collection of Dick Whetstone and the memories of the late Bill Manley to present a portrait of the northern part of the borough, Stoke Newington, Stamford Hill and Upper Clapton. The first selection, published in 1989, covered the whole borough before 1914. The second, in 1991, again ranged across all of LB Hackney, from 1890 to 1960. This book concentrates on the northern area of Hackney, including the former metropolitan borough of Stoke Newington.

Stoke Newington became a borough at the same time as Hackney, in 1900, when it incorporated the former urban district of South Hornsey. This consisted of two blocks of land north of Green Lanes, and the Brownswood area of the present-day Hackney. The boundaries of the old parish of Stoke Newington ran along Ermine Street (now the A10) to the west (thus excluding what is now called Stoke Newington Common), and Green Lanes to the south and west; to the north, however, the divisions between Tottenham and Hackney were originally only marked by fields. The name was first recorded in Domesday in 1086 as Neutone, when there was a small Saxon settlement in extensive woodland; the prefix, Stoke, first appeared in 1274, and may refer either to the tree stumps of a later clearance or to a timber structure.

The principal settlements grew up around Newington Green (of which only the northern part is in Stoke Newington), Church Street and Ermine Street, which as it runs south through Hackney is respectively Stamford Hill, Stoke Newington High Street, Stoke Newington Road and Kingsland High Street. The woodlands had all gone by the mid-eighteenth century, by which time the parish was chiefly noted for its associations with nonconformity, patronized by some of the rich London merchants who had settled there. Building development was initially limited to the main roads, notably Church Street and the High Street. However, an Act of 1814, initiated by the Prebendary of St Paul's Cathedral, as lord of the manor, and influenced by the lessees of the manor, the Eade family, allowed longer leases to be granted and encouraged builders. Early developers included Thomas Cubitt, but there were still only 1,816 houses in the parish in 1871. In the following year the Great Eastern Railway completed its line to Enfield and opened Stoke Newington station just outside the parish. There followed substantial building development, much of it in the next fifteen years, so that by 1913 there were 7,962 houses in the borough. In turn, the social composition of the district changed from the mid-1880s, with the wealthy gradually moving out and poorer people coming in, especially to the southern parts. Older houses were turned into factories, as furniture and clothing industries were established in the area.

Clapton and Stamford Hill formed the highest parts of the parish of Hackney; the highest point on the road from London was at Stamford Hill near Portland Avenue, before it dropped down again into Tottenham. To the east the land fell away sharply at High Hill Ferry, and more gently down Spring Hill to the River Lea. Upper Clapton Road formed part of the route from Cambridge Heath to Stamford Hill, the division between Upper and Lower Clapton being regarded by the early nineteenth century as being the junction with the Lea Bridge Road. Here had once stood a royal palace, the Kings Place, later Brooke House. Lea Bridge Road had once been Mill Fields Lane, going to a ferry over the Lea; it became a turnpike road in 1757 when the first Lea Bridge was built. Both Stamford Hill and Upper Clapton were attractive locations for larger houses; Cedar House at the junction of the two roads seems to have been the first, dating from around 1760. A local landowner, Thomas Webbe, carried out some development at Clapton Common in the 1770s, and owned the industrial complex at the bottom of Spring Hill, which included a tile yard, calico ground, three wharves and a creek in 1774. There were also tile kilns on Spring Lane, but otherwise the area remained rural, with fine views out across the Lea valley. Stamford Hill proved popular as well, and by the 1820s a number of large houses had been built along its route. Wealthy residents included some of the mercantile Jewish community, including the Montefiores and the Rothschilds.

Hackney had been noted for its private schools since the 1630s and Samuel Pepys was a boarder in a Hackney school as a small child. Prior to the mid-nineteenth century most of these were in or near Mare Street and Lower Clapton Road, but as these areas became increasingly built up, the trade moved north and the large houses of Upper Clapton and Stamford Hill were ideally suited. The coming of the railway in 1872 provided the same stimulus to development as it did in Stoke Newington: the bulk of the road pattern for Stamford Hill was complete by 1894, and, with the creation of Springfield Park out of the grounds of three houses in 1906, Upper Clapton's initial development was mostly completed.

It is with this period that this book is mostly concerned, drawing in the main on postcards published from the late 1890s until the mid-1920s. There are some earlier images, including a small sample from that precursor of the postcard, Alfred Braddock, whose original card-mounted photographs of the 1880s were later reproduced as postcards as an early example of visual nostalgia. Postcard producers were useful; they photographed the newly built streets, and hoped to sell the postcards to the local residents. Much of this work must have been speculative; some would appear to have been direct commissions by individual householders or individual businesses. Main shopping streets would obviously sell well, and were common subjects. Sadly, from our point of view, the inhabitants of the crowded yards and courts off the High Street, at the back of Sandford Terrace or in the tiny streets at Big Hill, would have been seen as very poor customers. Commercial card makers did not venture into these areas and it was left to the photographers working for Hackney Borough Council to record their tenements prior to slum clearance in the 1930s.

If slums were to be cleared, then rehousing was needed, and this could be best achieved by clearing away larger houses and replacing them with new council estates. It was this process rather than the bombing of the Second World War that was to transform so much of Stamford Hill and Upper Clapton, and some of Stoke Newington. Many of the roads of the 1880s and 1890s survived, but the older houses on the main roads largely made way for the new estates, together with most of the property fronting the River Lea, cleared on the grounds that it was at risk through flooding. For those who have only known Stamford Hill and Upper Clapton after the 1950s, it is the views of the main roads that will present the biggest surprises.

Bill Manley provided the original text for the Stoke Newington part of this book. In editing and expanding his book to include parts of Hackney, I have tried to ensure that the building dates of properties in the pictures are included where possible and relevant. For the Stoke Newington parts of the book, these are based on the thorough research of the *Victoria County History of Inner Middlesex*, vol. 8, which includes the history of Stoke Newington. Dates for Upper Clapton and Stamford Hill houses are mostly drawn from the drainage records held at Hackney Archives Department. After 1856 any new connection to the sewerage system had to be approved by the local authority, and applications distinguish between existing houses and new developments. The date of an application does not guarantee an exact building date, but building would normally follow within six months for small developments and within eighteen months for larger ones. Where I believe that development was not immediate, I have given a later date. However, without exact evidence from photographs and other sources, precise dating is not possible. Even within these limits, this book should prove a useful guide to all those interested in dating a house, whether for commercial or personal interest.

David Mander

CHURCH STREET

The area now covered by Stoke Newington included a separate local authority of South Hornsey prior
to 1900, which was responsible for Brownswood, half of Clissold Park, most of the 'Poet' roads
north of Matthias Road, land between Nevill, Dynevor, Brighton and Stoke Newington Roads and a
narrow sliver on the west side of Albion Road near Newington Green. In 1881 this tiny authority
built itself new vestry offices on the site of the former Congregational Church and School on the west
side of Milton Road and these were taken over by Stoke Newington when it was made into a borough
and absorbed South Hornsey in 1900. By the time this view of the early 1930s had been posted,
Stoke Newington had built new offices on the site of Church Row, which opened in 1937. The
Milton Grove building was replaced by flats before 1970, though it is still commemorated by Town
Hall Approach, which runs from Albion Road past the north side of the site.

St Mary's old church on the north side of Church Street in a view by Alfred Braddock taken in the 1890s, and with one of the obliging policemen who often appear to provide foreground. The spire was an addition in 1829, during the last year of the rector, Dr Gaskin. His funeral service was preached by the curate, Augustus Clissold, who was later to court and marry the Crawshay heiress and give his name to the Crawshay estate, which then became known as Clissold Park. The church is now without its nineteenth-century north aisle, which was bomb damaged in 1940.

Stoke Newington's first war memorial was erected in the grounds of the new church. This view, looking west, also includes part of Park Crescent in the background. In June 1923 a memorial hall was opened next to the library to commemorate those who had served in the First World War.

The new church of St Mary, designed by George Gilbert Scott, was consecrated on 25 August 1858. Built on the site of the old rectory, the tower was raised and the spire added in 1890. This view was taken in 1936, for behind the war memorial cross the new town hall can be seen during the course of construction. The man in the peaked cap sold ice-cream from his tricycle, which had a three-note dulcimer fitted to attract customers, and was the forerunner of the modern ice-cream van.

The combined St Mary's churches' team of four ministers in 1904. Rector William Bryant Salmon, then newly appointed, had previously served at the London Mission to Seamen and St Leonard's, Shoreditch, and took over from Prebendary Leonard Shelford as Rector and Surrogate Rural Dean of Hackney and Stoke Newington. He was to remain for fourteen years and had three assistants. Francis Edward Birch was newly ordained, and Francis William Reginald Holmes had served at St James's, Clapton, and in Australia prior to his appointment in 1902. He left in 1907, taking on the parish of Bowes Park. Stanley Power had also come in 1902 and was also to leave in 1907 to become Rector of St Barnabas's, Homerton. The team was ably supported by James Matthews, the choirmaster, who travelled from Richmond for fifty years and retired in 1918.

The western part of Church Street was called Paradise Row and it fronted on to the New River as it wound its way round the southern edge of the Crawshay estate. Fifteen of the houses in Paradise Row were built between 1721 and 1764. This view looking east is another by Alfred Braddock and was taken in 1879. The houses nearest the camera replaced an earlier house prior to 1845. Just visible at the end of the row is a house once occupied by William Wrighton, a composer of drawing-room ballads, and beyond again is the tower of St Mary's Church, as it appeared before the spire was added. Paradise Row residents included several members of the Hoare family of merchants and bankers. Samuel Hoare and his brother-in-law Joseph Woods, another resident of the row, were active in the campaign to abolish slavery in the late 1780s. William Wilberforce was a frequent visitor.

Paradise Row, looking west in 1886, a Braddock view. Stoneleigh House, behind the boys, was the residence of chemical manufacturer William Hanbury. Today only five houses remain (including the bay-fronted one).

At the end of Paradise Row the New River turned south, and this view of 1930 shows Park Lane Bridge, taken a year before road widening and alterations obliterated the bridge. To the right is Williams Brothers Direct Supplies Stores and ahead are the last houses in Park Lane by the junction with Carysfort Road. After 1946 the New River terminated at the Green Lanes Pumping Station, and by 1952 only a trace of the New River remained, just to the east of the former bridge.

The view from Park Lane Bridge looking south-west, *c.* 1910. Beyond the house on the corner of Park Lane can be glimpsed parts of Aden Terrace. Today these houses look out over allotments that have replaced the culverted New River.

Church Street from just beyond Edwards Lane, looking west, in a view by C. Degan of 1923. A game of hide-and-seek is in progress outside the Memorial Hall, which had just opened. The ivy did a great deal to soften the brick gables of the original public library building of 1892. During the Second World War there was another attempt to disguise the red brickwork – this time with camouflage paint.

Another Degan card from 1923, looking east. Four shops, converted from houses in Church Row, were demolished to make way for the library; Henry Taylor's chemist shop survived until 1922 when it was cleared to make way for the Memorial Hall. On the other side of the road, Isaac Mallin's oil shop traded for the first twenty or so years of the twentieth century and then continued in other hands, while Agate & Co. used No. 183 Church Street for its piano-making business from 1885 to 1957.

Church Row on the right and Sisters Place on the left, *c.* 1911. Church Row consisted of nine houses which were built on the site of the Manor House between 1695 and 1700, mostly by Job Edwards. By 1911 the Row was owned by Wynne Baxter, JP and local coroner, who lived at No. 170 Church Street – part of the Row. On the death of Wynne's son – Francis William Baxter, the antiquarian – in 1932, Church Row was purchased by the Council and demolished for the construction of the Town Hall. Sisters Place had been built opposite by Edward Newens between 1715 and 1717 and acquired its name in 1813, when it was inherited by four sisters. Two houses have now had their shop-fronts removed and the original eighteenth-century frontages restored. Beyond the next terrace is the Rose and Crown, which was demolished along with Halstead House beyond it in 1930. The present Rose and Crown was then built on part of the Halstead House site, allowing Albion Road to be widened.

The west side of Albion Road, looking back towards the Church Street junction, *c.* 1905. In 1814 the Prebendary of St Paul's was persuaded by the lessees of the manor, the Eades, to obtain an Act of Parliament, which allowed the creation of leases for terms of years long enough to attract builders. One who did so was Thomas Cubitt, who bought plots on the newly laid out Albion Road in 1822 and developed them over the next seventeen years. This row survives today, although it is in rather poor condition.

Stoke Newington Borough Council had opened slipper baths in Milton Road in 1909 and Church Street in 1925, but the inhabitants had to wait until April 1930 for their first swimming pool. It was opened at the top end of Clissold Road by His Royal Highness, Prince George, who was later Duke of Kent and was killed in an air crash in the Second World War. This postcard must date from shortly after the opening. An adjoining hall of remembrance dates from fifteen years later. The virtually car-free streets of the time emphasize the presence of the lone open-topped car.

Carysfort Road, looking west towards the junction with Park Lane, c. 1910. Laid out in 1893, the smart red-brick terraces were completed within the year and the road has kept its appearance of a hundred years ago.

Albion Road from Albion Parade, in a Charles Martin view of around 1905, with a horse bus heading south. This is the point at which the northern part of Albion Road joins Park Lane (now Clissold Crescent) to form a huge semi-circle. To the left is the Albion Cigar Store. On the right, in front of the pillar-box and painted the same red colour, is a Saunders & Brown fire-alarm. Introduced in the 1880s, these provided a link to the fire station. In the event of fire the resident broke the glass to get at the alarm and then waited until the fire-engine arrived. Then there was the ride of a lifetime on the engine to reach the fire. Gradually ousted by the spread of private and public telephones, some of the Saunders & Brown alarms survived into the 1950s.

The Albion Cigar Store, half hidden by the Favourite horse bus from Victoria, in March 1904. The Imperial Theatre, advertised on the bus's side, stood opposite Westminster Abbey and moved to Canning Town two years later when the Westminster site was taken for the Methodist Central Hall. The large red diamond on the back of the bus is not an indication of the status of the driver, but an advert for Carter's Liver Pills. The Albion Hotel on the corner of Clissold Road has survived, though in not quite so imposing a style as it had ninety years ago.

Clissold Road, looking north from the Park Lane junction, *c.* 1910. Clissold Road (originally named Park Road) was laid out between 1850 and 1853 on former glebe land, and the houses in this view were built by Charles Birch and other builders between 1853 and 1855.

Moving day for the Geary family in 1911. 'Just surviving in a frightful muddle, hope to get straight some day,' reads a note on the address side!

Albion Parade, in an Alfred Braddock view of 1884, looking north from the Triangle, shortly after the terrace on the left had been built. The Albion Cigar Stores is on the right behind the trees and the other side of the road is still open land. The delivery boy, who may have come from one of the shops in Allen Road, looks at the camera as the first cart pulls over to let the second pass.

The same scene in a Charles Martin view of around 1907. The houses on the right have lost their gardens and bow windows and the other side of the road now has shops, the nearest to the camera being J. Wells Woods's chemist's shop. Four years later Henry Harris's oil shop at No. 4 Albion Parade was replaced by the Albion Picture Palace; now shoppers could also be entertained.

The Triangle, as seen from Park Lane (Clissold Crescent), in another Charles Martin view of 1907. The little terrace included a laundry, dairy, hairdresser and a milliner. On the left is Herbert Joseph Shackell's off-licence, and the large block on the right is Connaught Mansions.

The Triangle, looking south down Albion Road, with an obliging posing policeman, c. 1910. The middle house on the right-hand side is marked with a cross on the original card and the sender has written: 'You will see what a lovely place I live in . . .'

The Red Lion on the north side of Church Street stands at the junction with Lordship Road and Red Lion Lane. This Alfred Braddock photograph was taken around 1910. First recorded in 1697, the Red Lion had the parish lock-up, stocks, pound and whipping-post at the rear. An engine house was added and the early nineteenth-century lock-up and engine house still survive. The pub was demolished in 1924 and its modern replacement, since renamed the Magpie and Stump, stands a little further back from the road.

Church Street, Stoke Newington. No. 1899.

Church Street, looking east from the junction with Bouverie Road, *c.* 1922. On the left the trees mark the southern gate of Abney Park Cemetery and the former site of Abney House. On the right the portico belongs to Abney Park Congregational Church. Abney Chapel had its origins in meetings that took place in 1662. The first chapel, built after 1672, was demolished to make way for Abney House in around 1700. Thereafter, the congregation worshipped in a small building near Barn Street, where Isaac Watts the hymn writer was a preacher. The new chapel in this view – with seats for 1,000 people – was built in 1838, the portico was added in 1862, and further extensions were made in 1869 and 1877. Badly damaged in the Second World War, it was replaced by a smaller brick church on the same site in 1957.

The eastern end of Church Street from just beyond Lancell Street. Traffic is scarce enough to allow the camera to be set up in the middle of the road – the 'B' type bus on route No. 27 to Twickenham can easily avoid the photographer. Shops in this area included Uffel the stationers, another local postcard publisher, and Weeden's oil shop, now an Indian restaurant.

Although labelled Nevill Road by Charles Martin, this 1906 view actually shows only the southern part of the road, with Wordsworth Road continuing on where the wagons are grouped. Prior to 1861 this was Cut Throat Lane; Wordsworth Road was created in that year and Nevill Road followed in 1870. Today the shops on the left have been replaced by Butterfield Park, named after William Butterfield, architect of St Matthias Church, which can just be seen in the distance, beyond Wordsworth Road school. The church was sponsored by Dr Robert Brett and was completed in 1854, with Thomas Alder Pope as the first incumbent. The first organist, William Henry Monk, compiled *Hymns Ancient and Modern*, which included 'Evening', the best-known setting of 'Abide with Me', and was published in 1861.

St Faith's Church stood on the corner of Knebworth and Londesborough Roads, also built under the patronage of Dr Brett. It replaced the original iron church, and Dr Brett lived to see the church completed in 1873, when the consecration service was an occasion of a ritualist demonstration by eighty priests in surplices. When a newly appointed vicar, in obedience to his bishop, tried to revoke the ritualistic practices, he provoked a storm of protest and the resignation of the entire choir. The High Church won the day. This view shows the Easter decorations of 1909, during the incumbency of C.H.V. Pixell.

St Faith's Church during the Harvest Festival of 1909. St Faith's congregation declined between the wars, with competition from Nonconformist churches, an increased Jewish presence in this area of Stoke Newington, and general indifference. All but the shell of the church was destroyed by a V-1 flying bomb in 1944, and the parish was later amalgamated with that of St Matthias. The site is now covered by a block of flats, Londesborough House.

NEWINGTON GREEN

Only the north side of Newington Green lay within the parish of Stoke Newington and it is first recorded by
name in 1480. Originally 'a most rude wilderness with large old trees', the green was railed in and improved
in 1742. Newington Green Unitarian Chapel, whose congregation originated in the 1660s, was built in 1708.
By 1761 Newington Green was described as a pleasant village, with well-built houses and a row of trees on
either side. Famous inhabitants included Daniel Defoe, who married a local girl in 1684 and tried to raise civet
cats here in 1692. Abraham Price, the first English wallpaper maker (who died in 1756), had a house here,
and the philosopher John Stuart Mill spent a happy three years of his childhood here from 1810 to 1813.
Dr Brett, the High Churchman, was a mid-Victorian resident. Changes were under way at the end of the
nineteenth century, however, and in 1892 an old three-storey house on the corner of Albion Road was
demolished to build the Italianate bank, which was in use by the National & Provincial at the time of this view
of around 1910. By 1929 all the buildings on the north side except the church were in commercial use.

Albion Road, looking towards Newington Green from just south of Connaught Mansions, in July 1931. The houses on the left date from the 1850s, those on the right from the 1880s. The light-coloured house was owned by John Waddington's, which printed playing cards, theatre programmes and board games. Their most famous product, Monopoly, appeared shortly after the date of this card. In the distance the small-wheeled vehicle may well be an organ-grinder, rattling out 'Goodnight Sally' or 'On the Sunny Side of the Street'.

Closer still to the Green, this is the section of Albion Road near Lavell Street, a Charles Martin view of 1907, looking north. There are some additional shops and the gas lamps have gone, but otherwise there have been few changes to this scene.

The flags are out for the Silver Jubilee of George V on the Mildmay Club on the north side of Newington Green in 1935. The Mildmay Radical Club and Institute was founded on 18 August 1888 in Newington Green Road, moving to the Green in 1894, when the vicar of St Matthias's attacked the club for its pernicious influence among the young. This building, designed by architect member Alfred Allen, had its foundation stone laid on 27 October 1900 and, unusually, the architect also helped with the financial arrangements. The club changed its name in 1930 when it ceased to be political, and still flourishes today.

Alfred Braddock photographed a very different Newington Green in 1889 from our first view, on p. 31. Newington Green Unitarian Chapel was refronted in 1860, when the congregation's affairs were directed by the energetic treasurer, Andrew Pritchard. Church Walk, alongside the chapel, led to two houses – Howard and Warwick houses – built in 1854 on the site of two earlier nineteenth-century cottages. The two houses on the corner with Albion Road dated from the mid-eighteenth century and were demolished when Albion Road was widened in 1892. The East Highbury Liberal Club had a brief existence on the Green from 1888 to 1890.

Springdale Road, seen here in September 1929, was originally called Aden Grove North, as it was next along from Aden Grove. Laid out by 1868, the houses were built in 1871–3. All is quiet, but for a solitary car and a lady petting a dog.

Green Lanes looking north from the Royal Oak public house in 1922. Allardyce's, on the corner of Springdale Road, formed part of a chain of bakery stores; this branch ran a sub-post office. Beyond is Egeleton's oil shop, Jeans' drapers, the Mayfield Laundry, Godfrey's butcher's shop and Robert Robinson's confectioner's shop. On the left is the spur for Leconfield Road. Green Lanes Wesleyan Church, built in 1874, had lost its spire after storm damage in 1920; it was destroyed by fire in 1968 and replaced by the present brick building. The Moorgate-bound No. 41 tram has just entered the short stretch of single-line track at the corner of Burma Road, which doubles again just in front of the camera.

A Charles Martin view of 1906, looking south along Green Lanes from the Church Street junction. The shoppers on the left are just outside the chemist's shop. These shops, together with the adjoining Newington Hall Villas in Church Street and the other houses at the rear in Statham Grove, were built in 1876–7 on the site of Newington Hall, a large classical style house of the 1820s. This was the work of Benjamin Massey, who also built Paradise Place, the row of houses behind the trees on the left. Beyond is the intact spire of Green Lanes Wesleyan Church and the houses in Petherton Road, which follows the course of the covered New River on its way to Canonbury.

Fort House and Melrose House, on the Islington side of Green Lanes and numbered 173–5, had become St Andrew's, by the time of this 1923 view. In 1920 the pair had been purchased by the Church Missionary Society, and was originally used for men. It was used for women from the end of 1922 until 1934, when the men returned and stayed until the outbreak of the Second World War. A block of flats now occupies this site, but an identical pair survive to the south and have just been restored.

Petherton Road, looking north to the truncated Green Lanes Methodist Church, in the mid-1920s. This end of the road, all of which lies within Islington, was completed in 1882.

Section Three

BROWNSWOOD AND MANOR HOUSE

A London County Council 'E1' class tram pauses by the request stop in Green Lanes at the gates of Lordship Park, just south of the 1854 pumping station, in 1924. To the west lay Brownswood Park, the largest part of South Hornsey prior to its absorbtion into Stoke Newington in 1900. The 'E1's were introduced in 1908 and were replaced on the No. 41 route by trolleybuses before 1939, though route No. 35, which also used Green Lanes, continued to have trams until around 1952. Brownswood Park was home to merchants, professionals and those living on rents and dividends.

Green Lanes, looking south from below the Pumping Station towards the Lordship Park junction, *c.* 1900. The railings of the filter beds of 1852 are to the right. Apart from the lack of traffic, this view has changed little in ninety-five years, although the coming development of the filter beds was soon alter this area of Green Lanes substantially.

Lordship Park Green Lanes Stoke Newington.

The Green Lanes end of Lordship Park in 1905, with a horse bus from Stoke Newington Common on its way to Finsbury Park. Lordship Park was planned as an extension from Manor Road to Green Lanes as early as 1855, but work did not start until after 1864, with the majority of the houses built through the remainder of the decade by Thomas John Angell. The lion and griffin on the gateposts were repeated as occasional motifs in the houses along the road and a few still survive. Only the lion is still intact at the end of the road and the inner of the two sets of gateposts has been removed for road widening.

Finsbury Park Road formed part of the development of Brownswood in the late 1860s. This view of around 1910 was taken from the junction with Somerfield Road looking north towards the Finsbury gate of Finsbury Park.

Wilberforce Road lies parallel and to the east of Finsbury Park Road, and was in the course of being laid out in 1871. The church on the right is Wilberforce Road Wesleyan Methodist Church. Founded in 1871, this building replaced an iron church in 1875. A church hall was added in 1901.

Seven Sisters Road, seen from near the Finsbury gate, in 1933. The parade of shops on the right replaced the mostly residential Cumberland Terrace not long before 1925, offering two floors of retail space to prospective businesses. Beyond them is Wilberforce Road Wesleyan Church, whose fine proportions can be appreciated in this view. The church was demolished in the 1960s and replaced by the present yellow-brick building.

St Andrew's Road was quiet and empty, but for a few children, when this view looking north towards the junction with Paget Road was taken around 1905. The road was one of William Osment's projects and the houses were built from 1887.

For once it was the dog that did not stand still. This is Springdale Road, looking west towards Green Lanes from the bend. The houses date from the early 1880s.

Brownswood Bowling Club had been founded in 1871 and initially used a small triangle of land at the back of the houses fronting on to Green Lanes, Queens Road and Kings Road (now Kings Crescent). By 1901 the club prowess was such that it took on a touring Australian side and, to cries of 'Cooee', rolled on to victory. In 1911 the club moved to more spacious premises at No. 256 Green Lanes and this view shows part of the grounds, with the New River and the West reservoir in the background. Here the club was able to offer croquet, tennis, bowls, archery and putting, and provide a pavilion and tearoom. The club survived until 1940, when the site was purchased for the new Woodberry Down estate.

Two Metropolitan Electric Tramway Company trams wait at Manor House, *c.* 1904. Horse trams had reached Manor House in 1885 and were extended on to Wood Green two years later. The line had been acquired by the North Metropolitan Tramway Company in 1892, which sold the route on to the Metropolitan Electric in 1904. It was this company, as its name implies, that electrified the line. Car No. 9 is about to swing into the terminus in the middle of the road, while Car No. 10 is bound for Wood Green. The public house was built in 1832 and Stoke Newington's local governing body, the vestry, chose to meet there for a number of years.

'An orchestra every evening' is on offer in 1928 at the Manor House, which still has its board boasting of a brief stop by Queen Victoria. The public house had its own concert room which was licensed from 1852 to 1903 and which clearly survived in use thereafter. The old building was rebuilt in 1930. The policeman has just stepped back to allow the lorry and the 'NS' type buses on route No. 29 to move off; squeezed in between is a single-decker on route No. 538 from Forty Hill to Stroud Green.

The long, straight Queens Road (now Queens Drive) was laid out in the 1860s and this is the section to the north of the Brownswood Road junction. It was at No. 123 that Walter Macqueen-Pope, the theatre manager and critic, spent his childhood. He dubbed Queens Road the 'best' road, with this part of the road being the best of the best – an opinion borne out by modern research into the census of 1881. Six houses in this part of the road, including No. 123, were destroyed in the bombing raid of 7 September 1940 and St Johns Court now occupies the site.

Section Four

LORDSHIP PARK

Lordship Road, looking north from the corner with Manor Road, on a postcard by Martin

Sander, c. 1906. The little boy has left the nursemaid to attend to his model engine, while

the law stands by. On the corner is the Manor Road Presbyterian Church, which was built

in 1884 and was demolished and replaced by a smaller building in 1971.

The junction of Seven Sisters Road (to the left) and Woodberry Down, in a view taken by local postcard publisher G. Smith in around 1900. On the right through the trees is the first Marlborough House, which was built in 1821 and was to last for just over a hundred years. Through the trees in the centre is St Olave's Church, built in 1894, taking its name, pulpit and font from the City church of St Olave, Old Jewry, which was demolished in 1888–9. The two carts by the lamp-post have stopped to allow the horses to take water from a drinking trough. On the far left the man may be leading a supplementary horse, slipped from the horse tram in the distance, and he and the horse will be going back to the depot, just round the corner.

The New River, looking west from Lordship Road bridge, *c.* 1904. The workman on the left may be one of the Walksmen, whose duties included weeding the river once a week. The West Reservoir of 1831 is on the left and to the right are the grounds of Queen Ann Lodge, home of Sir John Johnson Runtz, first mayor of Stoke Newington.

There has been a fine turn out for Alfred Braddock in this view of part of Fairholt Road, *c.* 1905. The camera is looking east towards Bethune Road, with the spire of St Andrew's Church of 1884 in the distance. Fairholt Road was mostly the work of one of the largest builders operating in the area, William Osment of Palatine Road, and these houses dated from 1881 to 1885.

St Kilda's Road, looking east from the junction with St Andrew's Road towards Bethune Road, *c.* 1904. The houses were the work of another prolific local builder in 1880, Edward Paget Nunn, who lived in nearby Lordship Park. The name may echo the Scottish association of nearby St Andrew's Road.

This Alfred Braddock view of 1879 shows Lordship Road from what will be the junction with St Kilda's Road, looking north. On the left are the railings and walls of large houses that were built in the 1840s. The other side of the road was mostly fields, though there are a further couple of houses beyond the bend. However, Lordship Road – once Lordship Lane, and in existence by 1649 – was about to be transformed.

The building development of the early 1880s covered the fields to the left, but Lordship Road still looked well wooded in this postcard view by James Uffell of Church Street, which dates from around 1905. The left-hand side of the road was altered after the Second World War by the construction of the Bearsted Memorial Hospital in 1947 and the Lordship South Estate to the north, which was completed in 1959. The hospital closed in 1983.

Woodberry Down was created under the Act of 1814, initially running from Green Lanes to Lordship Road. In 1868 it was extended from the junction with Lordship Road to meet the newly created Bethune Road, running north of the course of the New River and the East Reservoir and crossing the river near Bethune Road. Building started on the south side in the late 1860s. The Thatched Cottage – a medium-sized house built shortly before 1825, with grounds running down to the New River – was replaced by the mid-1880s by a house called Grasmere, seen on the right-hand side of this view.

Whoever took this photograph left little record, but from a pencil note linking it to Lordship Road and map evidence, this is likely to be Linton Lodge, one of the houses built on the west side of Lordship Road a little to the north of the junction with Grayling Road. It dates from the 1820s and had an extensive garden. In the 1880s it was owned by John Runtz, before he moved up the road to Queen Ann Lodge. Linton Lodge – later numbered No. 65 – was acquired, along with the house to the north, by the Jewish Secondary School Movement in 1947 for the Avigdor School and had been demolished by 1959.

Rose and Norman Wickes pose either side of the gateway of their house, No. 36 Allerton Road, in 1922, shortly after their move from Forburg Road. This was one of a pair of houses on the north-west side whose gardens backed on to the pumping station on Green Lanes. The road was developed by William Hardy and the houses were built between 1882 and 1888. The western entrance had originally been an access way to the stables behind the houses in Lordship Road; the name is taken from Richard Allerton, one of three surveyors responsible for local maps in the 1840s.

Manor Road was created shortly before 1827, though building was largely confined to its eastern end until the mid-1870s, and as late as 1874 the road was still private with tolls levied on animal traffic. The majority of houses in this Charles Martin view of 1907, taken from the Lordship Road junction, were the work of Thomas Bricknell and William Osment. St Andrew's parish had a temporary church here from 1876 to 1884; the church in this view is the Presbyterian one seen earlier.

A very quiet Lordship Road basks in the afternoon summer sun in this view of around 1905, looking north not far from the junction with Lordship Grove, which is just visible behind the woman on the left. Six cottages, built before 1837, are on the left behind the trees; the terraces to the right date from the early 1860s. In the distance the junction with Grazebrook Road is just visible on the left-hand side, before the bend; this was built over part of the Hackney Brook. Lordship and Oak Houses cover the left-hand side of the road today.

An arboreal view of the section of Queen Elizabeth's Walk near the entrance to Grazebrook Road, with Clissold Park on the left. This is an example of Martin Sander's work of around 1910. The Walk was probably formed in the early eighteenth century from ground used as a public walk from the houses in Church Row – there is no known association with the Tudor monarch.

Nurseryman William Martin and his family have decorated their house, No. 52 Bouverie Road, for the coronation of King George V and Queen Mary in 1911. Bouverie Road was laid out by John Rodda in 1859 and the houses were built during the next decade. From local directories it appears that William had inherited the house from his father, George, who was resident there in the mid-1880s, trading as a florist. This card was sent by hand to Mrs Roberts in Tottenham by Rosie – perhaps the woman who poses by the front gate?

Section Five

CLISSOLD PARK

Clissold House was a private house in Newington Park when Alfred Braddock took this view

of the west front in 1879. The park was put together by Jonathan Hoare, a merchant, who

had previously lived in Paradise Row, opposite. He demolished four houses that used to stand

on the north side of Church Street and had this house, designed by his nephew Joseph Woods,

built on the site of one in 1790. The brick earth for the house came from the estate and the

excavated areas later became lakes. Hoare's financial difficulties forced him first to mortgage

and then sell the estate and it passed to Thomas Gudgeon in 1800, who in turn sold it to

William Crawshay, from the iron-making family. It was William Crawshay's daughter,

Eliza, who fell in love with curate Augustus Clissold and married him on her father's death

in 1835. Although the estate reverted back to the Crawshay family in 1882 on Clissold's

death, it was his name that was firmly linked with the estate.

115140.　Clissold Park. N.

By the spring of 1927 little seems to have changed, other than the addition of some railings, but the house now forms refreshment rooms for a municipal park. The Crawshay family sold the house to the Ecclesiastical Commissioners in 1886. The commissioners intended to parcel it up for building development, but in the face of a vigorous campaign led by Joseph Beck and John Runtz, they relented. The Metropolitan Board of Works and Stoke Newington Vestry stepped in and purchased the estate, helped by funds from three other neighbouring local authorities, and it opened to the public on 24 July 1889.

115142. Clissold Park. N.

Another view from 1927 shows how popular Clissold Park was with local people. In front, just below the spire of St Mary's Church, is an aviary. London County Council, which ran the park, made it one of the first in London to have birds and animals. Sadly neither the LCC or Stoke Newington would fund the conversion of the house to a museum.

The lakes in the estate had been filled in prior to the sale and had to be re-excavated before the park opened. They were named after the leaders of the campaign, the western one becoming Beckmere and the eastern Runztmere, although the names did not persist in common use. This is the southern edge of Beckmere looking towards the park lodge on Green Lanes in around 1905, prior to the introduction of boats. The swans also have no competition from the postwar introduction of Canada geese. The land behind the screen of trees was used for a barrage balloon in the Second World War.

This view, dating from 1923, may well have been taken during the first season that boats were brought back after the First World War. This is the north side of Beckmere looking east. Both Dick Whetstone and Bill Manley were visitors to the park as boys – one was fascinated by the paddleboats, but the other preferred to bike along the secluded paths behind the lakes, disturbing courting couples.

The Lodge, Clissold Park, from the Green Lanes entrance, *c.* 1907. Built in the early 1890, the lodge was backed by the Stroud brothers' plant nursery, until it was replaced by the Clissold Court flats in 1936.

Although this view was taken in the late 1920s, the scene could have been recorded at any time during the last one hundred and fifty years. This is part of the surviving stretch of the New River in Clissold Park, looking towards the house from the old bridge leading to the deer pens. Behind, on the left, is the old embankment at the top end of Lower Meadow, but the corresponding part of the river and the bridge have gone.

A fallow deer stag in the enclosure, in the mid-1920s. From the early days donations to the park's collection of livestock were encouraged and at one time visitors could see guinea pigs and wallabies. The deer remain a feature of this and other North London parks today.

Exotic life forms have sprung from the shrubbery in the line of duty. The police regularly patrolled the park and this pair have been caught in a Rapid Photo postcard of around 1907 at the edge of the deer pens, with the spires of the old and new churches behind them.

The aviary is to the right and the deer pens are straight ahead in this view of around 1928. The aviary was moved from this position after the war.

The footbridge over the New River on a late summer afternoon in the 1930s. The two children are heading for one of the two Church Street exits. At that time the New River wound on to run alongside Paradise Row, behind the camera; today it stops short to form a wildlife pool.

Empire Day, held annually in May, was a great occasion in the school year. In 1902 local children were brought to Clissold Park to celebrate.

The wisdom of ages is being inspected outside Clissold House in 1930 and an unknown wit captioned the photograph: 'The Park Lane Parliament'. Fierce indeed, must have been those park bench debates . . .

THE LONDON ROAD

Stoke Newington Road and High Street both formed part of Ermine Street, known locally in the
sixteenth century as London Way, and part of a turnpike road from 1713 until 1865. Early
Hackney and Stoke Newington grew here – the parish border ran down the middle of the road. The
community was centred principally round the Church Street junction, but from the sixteenth century
there were also inns along the roads. Behind the tram in this view of around 1907 stands the Palace
Theatre, which seated 1,710 and was designed by Frank Matcham (the architect of the Hackney
Empire). It opened on 27 December 1897. It was a cinema from 1917 to 1920, and saw circus and
pantomime as well as films and drama. It was closed from 1935 to 1939, and after the war was
home to the New Yiddish Theatre Company, before closing altogether in 1950, when it was
demolished to make way for the Alexandra Court block of flats.

The entrance to Brighton Road from Stoke Newington Road, 1906. On one side is A.P. Barnard the chemist, with his ipecacuanha balsam cure for every ailment, and Henry Lovell's oil shop, with a fine display of hardware. In 1868 a house called Sisters Cottage fronted on to the road, with a field behind. Brighton Road had replaced both by 1878. The postcard was sent by Annie and Willie Little, who lived at No. 24, just beyond the bend.

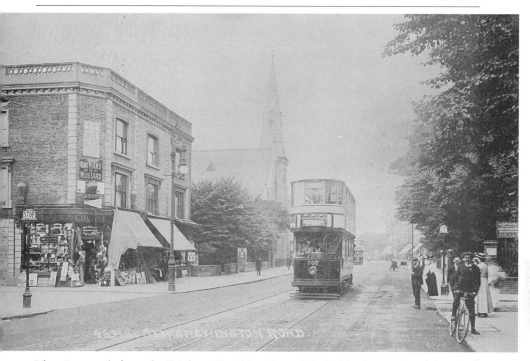

The view north from the Brighton Road junction of Stoke Newington Road, in a Bell card of around 1908. Just in case the unwashed have not got the message, Henry Lovell means to tell the world about soap. In the same parade are the Clarke brothers' draper's shop and Sidney Longhurst's sweet shop, while behind the seclusion of his trees is the mysterious John Cowlow Ash, 'inventor and patentee'. The spire belongs to Devonshire Square Baptist Chapel, which was founded in 1870 with the proceeds of the sale of the Devonshire Square Chapel in Bishopsgate Street. The lecture and classrooms to the south of the church were added in 1890. This building was damaged during the Second World War and was rebuilt afterwards. The foundation stones for both the chapel and the school survive on the site.

LONDON. Stoke Newington Road. No. 1392.

John Cowlow Ash and his neighbours were displaced before 1915 when their houses made way for the Apollo Cinema, the round domes of which can be seen beyond Devonshire Square Baptist Church in this 1921 postcard. Baptists and cinema-goers may not have made good neighbours, especially when the Apollo proprietors tried periodically for a Sunday licence. The Apollo changed its name to the Ambassador in 1936 and then, after a brief period as a bingo hall, had a reincarnation as the Astra Cinema in 1974. It is now a mosque and there is a block of flats on the site of the church.

The tram tracks are very new in this view of the top end of Stoke Newington Road, taken around 1875, because construction had finished only three years before. West Hackney Church, consecrated in 1824, dominates the corner with Amhurst Road. To the south is the short-lived Tyssen manorial and estate offices, the domain of Chester Cheston. These were built shortly after 1868 and made way for three shops in 1880–1. The Tyssen family became lords of the various Hackney manors from the late seventeenth century and gradually expanded their holdings to become the largest landowners in Hackney. They were served by two generations of the Cheston family, who managed their Hackney estates, but Charles Cheston, the family solicitor, defrauded his employer, Lord Amherst, of £250,000. Cheston had also helped himself to the proceeds of an estate that Lord Amherst administered as a trustee. When Cheston died in 1906, a court case ensued, forcing Lord Amherst into selling his prized art collection and bringing on his death in 1909.

Opposite: the first Caledonian public house, which stood on the Hackney side of Stoke Newington Road, on the corner with Wellington Road, *c.* 1905. There had been a plant nursery here, run by the Ross family from around 1786 to 1840, and the pub took on the name of the nursery. It was rebuilt in 1885 and was bombed in the Second World War. A modern replacement moved a block further north to the corner of Somerford Grove. There is a story that a large figure of a Scotsman was carefully lifted down from a niche inside the building when the pub was cleared, but when the workmen returned from lunch it had been smashed to pieces.

The view up the road from the Walford Road junction in 1908. This area of South Hornsey formed part of the Walford family estate, and the road named after them was probably laid out shortly before the Walford public house was built in 1866. By 1908 the landlady was Mrs Rosa Melvina Busby, presumably the widow of G.C. Busby. The row of shops beyond includes West Hackney Church House. Today the Walford has been renamed Rumours and has lost its distinctive parapet names.

Another look at the Alexandra Theatre, in 1935, with buses, lorries and trams very much in evidence, but only two cars. On the right is part of the police court, dating from 1890. Behind the court the tangle of small streets was cleared in the 1930s for the Hindle House estate.

West Hackney Church around 1909, with two purple and cream trams passing, one about to enter Stoke Newington High Street. One of the original 'daughter' churches of St John at Hackney, it was badly damaged by bombing in September 1940. Its modern replacement of 1950, St Paul's Church, stands a little further back from the road.

C.H. Martin took over the Bon Marché drapery and furniture store in the early twentieth century from Emery and Crawford. They had established it in the late 1890s in this row of shops that had replaced the former Coronation Place in 1885. It was a shop assistant who sent this wintery card to a woman friend in 1905. Perhaps the Bon Marché, like other stores of the period, used an overhead system of canisters on wires to transfer cash to the accounts section, a system in use in some department stores until the 1950s.

An almost traffic-free Stoke Newington High Street from the junction with West Hackney Church in 1930. There had been some hopes that the cupola and façade of the church could have been saved, but it was not to be. On the opposite side of the road was one of the grocery shops of Walton, Hassell and Port, and a few doors further on stuffed animals glared from the Lion Fur Stores (which features in *The London Borough of Hackney in Old Photographs 1890–1960*).

A peaceful haven at No. 17 Victoria Grove in 1908. Mrs Elizabeth Catford and her daughter are at the gate. Maybe some kind of business had been carried on from the house, judging from the board above the doorway, almost lost in the creeper, which might have dated from Henry Catford's time, prior to the mid-1890s. Dating from the mid-1860s, this house still survives today.

Electric trams were introduced on the route that included the London Road in 1907, and one is about to pass the Majestic Electric Palace Cinema in the High Street, 1923. C.H. Martin went into liquidation in 1910 and the whole row of shops was acquired by Electric Palaces Ltd, which built Amherst Hall Cinema Theatre in place of the last shop in the row, with an extension along the Batley Road frontage. The main attraction is the American film *The Swamp*, a rewrite of a recent British film *Broken Blossoms*, which starred Bessie Love and the Japanese Sessue Hayakawa, who was one of many stars to appear at the London Music Hall in Shoreditch in the same year. The Majestic later changed its name to The Vogue, specializing in continental films. Opposite is the bulk of the Stoke Newington police station of 1868, which was demolished in the late 1980s.

High Street, Stoke Newington.

The High Street, looking north from the junction with Victoria Grove (now Victorian Road) in 1908. Just beyond the carriage on the right is the junction with Hollar Road (then Union Street). George Elwood at No. 62 began as a stationers, probably shortly after this block had been built in the early 1890s, but by 1905 he had branched out into steam printing. Above Stewart's chemist's shop was one of Hackney's photographic studios. This view dates from around 1908, but it was posted to Germany in 1927 – so it was either very old stock or a reprint.

The High Street junction with Church Street, seen from the corner with Sanford Lane, in a Charles Martin card of 1907. On the opposite corner the Three Crowns (first recorded as the Fleur de Luce in 1603) was rebuilt in 1871 and again in 1898.

The White Hart, at No. 69 High Street, may have just acquired its new proprietor in this view of 1904, which almost certainly includes Charles August Steibritz – in the light-coloured coat – and some of his staff. The White Hart has changed sex over the years, for it was first recorded in 1625 as the White Hind. It was rebuilt after 1868, probably at the same time that the Victoria Grove area was being developed.

The High Street, a little to the north of the Dynevor Road junction, *c.* 1910. The postman is about to pass James Preston's butcher's shop, and in the distance, on the left-hand side just before the traffic jam of trams and carts, is the Rochester Castle public house. The pub was built by Richard Payne between 1801 and 1809 on the site of an earlier pub, the Green Dragon, which was mentioned in 1721. Payne came from Rochester, hence the pub name. It appears to have been rebuilt by 1894.

A little further up the road, this 1907 view was taken alongside Edwin Clarke's jeweller's and pawnbroker's shop at No. 124. Further up are Empress Teas and Robert Row's butcher's shop. The fire lamp is at the corner of Brooke Road and points to the nearby fire station. The 'E' class tramcar is in its first year of service.

Closer again to the Church Street junction is this 1904 view. On the left are Edwin Thomas Jarman's draper's shop at No. 135, Holdens tailor's shop and George Wallis, boot-maker to all the family. The tram track is single line in this part of the street. On the opposite side of the road the shops behind the Brooke Road fire sign are undergoing alterations; this row will shortly include the Maypole Dairy (see Section Eleven).

The view down Brooke Road from the High Street, in a Charles Martin card of 1907. The post office had been on the other side of the High Street by Dynevor Road at the end of the nineteenth century, but it had moved to join the sorting office by 1907. The fire station on the right was built in 1885 by Stimpson & Co. for £5,500, and was the successor to the earlier station next to the Methodist Church on the east side of the High Street. At that time the service was run by the Metropolitan Fire Brigade, but it was taken over by the London County Council in 1888, and it became the London Fire Brigade in 1904. Two years before, the Stoke Newington station was enlarged and it continued in service until 1974.

Stand by, Stoke Newington brigade! A steam fire engine, an escape ladder and a manual escape cart are on parade with their crews. This entrance was on Leswin Road, and the move from the High Street ensured that rapid departures would not be hampered by passing carts on the main road. After the 1974 move to Church Street, the station was used for three more years by the Kingsland brigade while their own station was being rebuilt. The bells, the top of the tower and the plaque have gone but the building still stands and is used for child welfare.

The Jolly Butchers public house, on the corner with Garnham Street, was rebuilt in 1896, around the same time as Garnham Street replaced the narrow tangle of houses and yards behind this part of the High Street. In this view of 1903, the pub sports a painting recalling the 1784 election antics of Georgina, Duchess of Devonshire, who was supposed to have kissed three butchers in Covent Garden, in exchange for their promise to vote for Charles James Fox. Butchers were common in this area of the High Street, and in 1910 a bull escaped from Mr Row's slaughterhouse and ran up the High Street. Halted by the sight of the Three Jolly Butchers – it was claimed – it made a dash for freedom on to Stoke Newington Common, which was transformed into a bullring during the efforts to catch it.

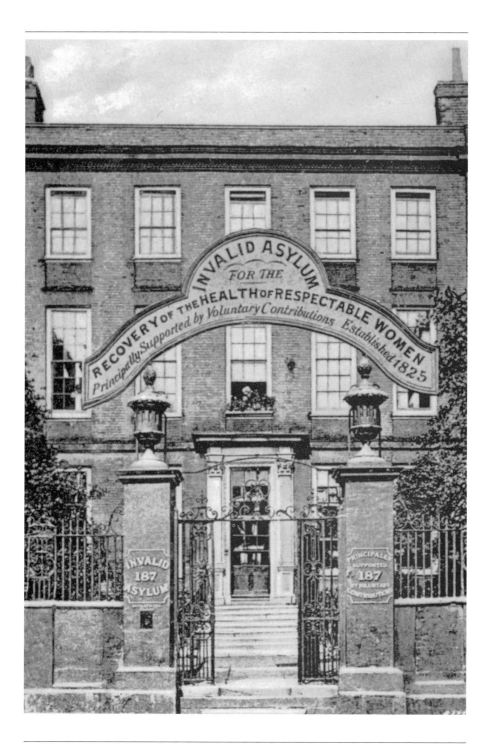

This group of three shops adjoined the High Street entrance to Abney Park Cemetery, and Dunkley's memorial mason's shop had occupied both Nos. 215 and 217 in the mid-1880s, before a succession of tearooms providing refreshment for visitors to the cemetery took over. Edwin Burr sold postcards as well as providing a circulating library. The shops probably date from around 1846.

Opposite: No. 187 High Street is one of a fine group of early eighteenth-century houses just north of the Church Street junction. Built in 1712, it was the home of wealthy Quaker, John Wilmer, from 1755 to 1764. Wilmer had a fear of being buried alive, and accordingly was interred in a vault in the garden, with a bell attached to his wrist! Used as a school after 1794, the house was taken over by the Invalid Asylum in 1830, who provided rest and medical care for domestic servants. Altered in 1909 to become the Stoke Newington home hospital for women, the institution moved to Stevenage during the Second World War and did not return. This view dates from around 1907.

The main gates to Abney Park Cemetery, with the avenue behind and the cemetery chapel spire rising above the trees, *c*. 1911. The cemetery was built in the grounds of Abney House, named after Sir Thomas Abney, a Bank of England director and Lord Mayor of London, who gained the property through marriage in 1700. It was acquired in 1838 by the Cemetery Company, whose principal was George Collison, son of a Nonconformist minister. The architect was William Hosking, though the lodges were designed by the Egyptologist, Joseph Bonomi. The first burial, of the Congregational minister of Upper Clapton Chapel, James Mather, took place in 1840.

The war memorial in Abney Park, seen here in the 1920s, was built over the catacombs. Behind the cross stands the statue of hymn writer Isaac Watts, who came for a brief visit to the Abney family and ended up staying for the last thirteen years of his life, dying in 1748. Abney House survived the loss of its grounds for only four years, before being demolished in 1843. Abney Park Cemetery suffered from bombing during the Second World War and progressive deterioration thereafter, until it was bought by Hackney Council for £1 in 1978. Today it is looked after by Abney Park Cemetery Trust.

Abney Park Cemetery took over from the closed Bunhill Fields as the principal Nonconformist burial ground in North London. Among the many famous interments are William and Catherine Booth and this was their monument as it appeared in the 1920s. The funeral cortège of General Booth in August 1912 was followed by an enormous procession of well-wishers and Salvation Army members, and was featured in *The London Borough of Hackney in Old Photographs before 1914*. Other famous names include James Braidwood of the London Fire Engine Establishment (who died in the Tooley Street fire of 1861), playwright T.W. Robinson (who died in 1871) and music-hall performer Albert Chevalier. Increasingly the economics of cemetery management forced the company to crowd graves in ever closer, as this view shows, and the imaginative planting scheme introduced in the 1840s was gradually lost.

St Michael and All Angels' Church, which stands at the corner of Northwold and Fountayne Roads, in 1905. Behind the lamp-post and the group of lounging boys is the vicarage. The children are all neatly dressed – has Sunday school just finished? As late as 1868 this area of Hackney was still rural, with Elm Lodge and its grounds to the south and Thornbury Park and Baden Farm to the north of Northwold Road. The site of the church was a small field on the edge of the large tree-nursery that was the principal employer of the area. The church was built in 1884–5, replacing a temporary iron church. This card was sent by one choir member to another in January 1906 to announce a practice session for 'Three for Jack', a new song made popular by Clara Butt's husband, Kennerley Rumford.

Northwold Road, looking east from the corner of Kyverdale Road, on a cold winter's day around 1905. The horse bus is heading towards Finsbury Park, with all its passengers inside avoiding the worst of the cold. The houses in this part of the road were built in 1880.

STOKE NEWINGTON COMMON

Stoke Newington Common, once Cockhanger Green and part of Hackney Parish, was originally bounded by the line of that part of Hackney Brook called The Old Brook to the north, the Tyssen estate boundary to the south and the small settlement that had spread from the High Street to the west. This included Sanford Terrace, which was built after 1776 by a brewer called Sandford. Kates Lane (later Northwold Road) and Shacklewell Lane (later Rectory Road) crossed the Common, as did an extension of Sanford Lane (now lost). The Common was curtailed by a new road to the south, and was bisected by the Great Eastern Railway in 1872. This introductory view shows Northwold Road, looking west towards the railway bridge around 1911.

'A piece of our rural village' was how the sender described this part of Stoke Newington Common, in a view taken around 1905 from the railway bridge looking east, showing the first houses in the road, built thirty years previously.

These are the shops on the curve of Amhurst Road, just beyond the junction with Shacklewell Lane, in the late 1920s. The post outside Eckers bakery is another fire alarm. These shops were built in 1866 and survive today.

Northwold Road by the Kyverdale Road junction again, this time around midday in an Edwardian summer.

Rectory Road, Stoke Newington N.

The junction of Amhurst and Rectory Roads, on a Charles Martin postcard, *c.* 1905. The Amhurst Arms marks the earlier end of Amhurst Road; the extension to Stoke Newington Road was built in the late 1860s. On the left is the Amherst Club, founded in 1885, whose premises were built in the early 1890s. In 1906 the club described itself as 'one of the cosiest, best appointed and most Up-to-Date Clubs in the Metropolis', and offered its members smoking concerts, cinderella dances, billiards, photography, chess, a masonic lodge and a library. However, it had been replaced by the North London Jewish Club by 1914, a sign of changing population in the area. Amhurst and Amherst both stem from the Tyssen family.

RECTORY ROAD "MEN'S OWN", STOKE NEWINGTON. N.

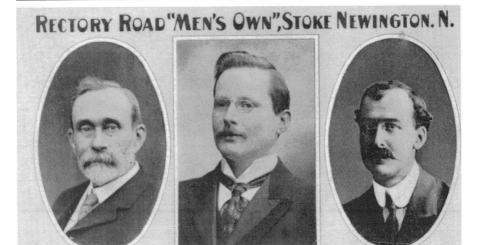

The local church played an important part in the social and religious life of the community in England before the First World War, and the active Rectory Road Congregational Church on the corner with Evering Road was no exception. Founded in 1865 in South Hornsey and moving to this site in 1882, church members founded the Hoxton Market Christian Mission in 1886. Closer to home, it had its own 'Men's Own' meetings. The Literary Society was probably founded around 1899, and these were the officers in 1904. The society offered a very active programme and was lucky to be able to book Mrs Kendal, later Dame Margaret Kendal. The previous year the star attraction had been G.K. Chesterton, who was notorious for turning up in the wrong place; hopefully the society was not disappointed.

RECTORY ROAD LITERARY SOCIETY, Stoke Newington, N. (opposite Rectory Rd. Station, G.E.R.)

LECTURES—SEASON 1906-7.

Thursdays.

Oct. 4.—Mr. EDWARD MINSHALL. Dramatic Recital.
  ,, 18.—Mr. F. ORMISTON-SMITH. Bioscopic Lecture—
      "Mountaineering in the Tyrol."
Nov. 1.—His Honour JUDGE WILLIS. "Milton: his Life
      and Writings."
  ,, 15.—Mr. CHARLES SAUNDERS, the Celebrated Tenor.
      Musical Chat: "The Songs we Love."
  ,, 29.—Professor BOTTOMLEY. "Microbes, Friendly and
      Otherwise." *(Limelight Views)*
Dec. 13.—Mr. A. B. MALDEN. "A Tour through the Italian
  1907. Cities." *(Cinematographic Views)*
Jan. 10.—Mrs. KENDAL. Dramatic Recital.
  ,, 24.—Rev. A. N. COOPER, the Walking Parson. "A Walk
      to Venice." *(Limelight Views)*
Feb. 7.—Professor HUBERT von HERKOMER, R.A.
      "England, Lovable and Paintable."
  ,, 21.—Mr. FRED. ENOCK, F.L.S., etc. "All Things
      Bright and Beautiful." *(Illustrated by Coloured
      Photography)*
Mar. 7.—Mr. ERNEST H. MILLS, the well-known Inter-
      viewer. "Peeps at Personalities." *(Limelight
      Views and Lightning Sketches)*
  ,, 21.—CONCERT by the LEONI LADIES' QUINTETTE.

RESERVED COURSE TICKETS, 7/6.
    UNRESERVED (Gallery except Front Row), 4/-

*Hon. Sec.—ALFRED WALMSLEY, 31, Northwold Road, Stoke
Newington Common, N.*

Agents—VALE'S LIBRARIES, 30, Stamford Hill, and 131, Stoke
Newington Road; Mr. BAXTER, 11, Northwold Road.

Doors open 7.40.   Lectures 8 p.m.

COPYRIGHT F. W. HART, LONDON.

Another Charles Martin view, this time looking north-east along Evering Road from near the Maury Road junction, *c*. 1905. The sailor suit of the little boy and the best dresses suggest Sunday visiting time; the houses again are just thirty years old.

Charles Martin took this view in the same summer, standing at the Brooke Road junction of Evering Road, looking towards the junction with Upper Clapton Road, beyond the bend. Some of the houses and all of the garden railings have gone – the latter for war salvage – but the view is recognizable today.

The top end of Benthal Road, looking north from the Brooke Road junction, *c.* 1906. Benthal Road was developed in 1875 and the houses were built two years later. It looks as if the small boy on the right has lost something – his marbles perhaps?

Benthal Road from the junction with Evering Road, looking north-west around 1904, with delivery boys attracting attention, and the houses on Stoke Newington Common in the far distance. This part of the road dates from 1882.

The Rendlesham Road end of Maury Road. William Hammer and his assistant have set their meat tables outside, while on the opposite side of the road Mr Talintyre's talents clearly extend beyond his prosaic directory listing of 'oilman', with groceries and colonial products on offer. Rendlesham Road dates from 1863 and there was a small group of shops in this part of the road from the late 1860s. By the early 1990s Hammer's had become a betting shop, and the shops and houses on the right were cleared to build Rendlesham House in the 1950s.

Maury Road, from the Common end, *c.* 1906. 'Ada', who sent the card, lived in the second tall house on the left. There are tower blocks on the corners of Brooke Road now, but the other houses, which date from 1882, are by the same builder as the top end of Benthal Road and are still there today.

The train approaching Stoke Newington station was bound for Liverpool Street, calling at Rectory Road, Hackney Downs, London Fields, Cambridge Heath and Bishopsgate. The engine is a James Holden Class 'S44' 0–4–4 tank in the royal blue livery of the Great Eastern Railway, hauling teak-coloured carriages. The thin pole visible over the bridge is a signal post, used to control the cross-over and siding alongside Manor Road. Prominent among the host of local tradesmen advertising on the platforms is Matthew Rose, on the left. This was the largest local department store, whose premises were on the corner of Amhurst Road and Mare Street.

Stoke Newington station opened to passengers in May 1872, and less than two months later services to the City were supplemented by a link at Edmonton Junction, enabling trains to reach Enfield Town. In November 1872 services were extended to Bishopsgate Lower Level and finally into the newly opened Liverpool Street station on 22 February 1874. We are looking south along Stamford Hill towards the High Street and the premises of Burr's library, which produced this card around 1905. More milk delivery is in progress as the horsemen ride north. Rigden Brothers had a draper's shop at No. 36 Stamford Hill.

STAMFORD HILL

Stamford Hill at the junction of Cazenove Road, c. 1920. The view has been taken from

alongside the Weavers' Arms, then in the hands of W.T. Booker. The most northerly part

of Hackney's section of the London Road was undeveloped before the seventeenth century,

with settlement concentrated by the ford near the Church Street junction. The higher

ground proved an attractive place to build houses for the rich, and development was under

way by 1740. The junction with Clapton Common had its own tollgate from 1713 to

take fees from those using the turnpike road, and a field just to the south had a gibbet to

display the remains of criminals executed at Tyburn in the 1740s.

Kelsey's Boots on the east side of Stamford Hill. At the end of this row of shops, dating from 1878, is Stoke Newington station, seen earlier. This row seems to have included a little of everything – general stores, a watchmaker, chemist, florist, post office, the vital servants' registry office (many houses would have had at least one domestic servant) and two midwives, who lived together over a sweetshop. From the later eighteenth century the road was lined with large houses and the wealthier residents included the Rothschilds. Changes to the area had begun before the coming of the railway in 1872, but this hastened Victorian development, including the building of shops and the gradual loss of the larger houses.

Still on the east side, we have moved north to the junction with Windus Road. The Bird Cage public house, under the management of W.R. Crystal in this view of around 1908, was first recorded in 1732. Windus Road began life as Bird Cage Walk, which continued as a footpath to join the present Oldhill Street en route to Clapton Common. The Bird Cage and the adjoining two shops were rebuilt in 1892; the remainder of the row dates from two years earlier. Horse buses and trams compete for custom, while Mr Rudolph has left his cart advertising his frame-making and cleaning services, perhaps to call on a client.

Opposite: another view of the Cazenove Road junction, around 1901–2, with horse buses waiting for custom and a sandwich-board man about to parade some deserving product along the road. The original Weavers Arms was replaced by this building in 1871, and the shops beyond date from 1875 to 1878.

Another photograph of Stamford Hill in around 1925, giving a better view of Stanley's circulating library. A General 'B' type bus on route No. 65 is parked in Windus Road between trips, and a nanny pushes her charge resolutely northwards.

The Convent of Our Lady of the Cenacle occupied Nos. 61–3 Stamford Hill, *c.* 1900. This was one of this Catholic order's four English convents, which hosted retreats and gave religious instruction. Both houses received additions in 1903 and 1906 but the Order moved to Hampstead around 1932. Shortly afterwards the houses were demolished for the construction of a Guinness Trust estate in 1933–4.

Even as late as 1910 this part of Stamford Hill still had the feeling of a spacious leafy past. This view taken in the early spring of 1907 shows the corner with Lynmouth Road on the right and a very new electric tram, introduced only a month or so before, heading south. The houses just visible probably date from around 1815, when Lynmouth Road was Grove Road, one of the few running through to Clapton Common. The road name changed in 1890. In the distance is the spire of Stamford Hill Congregational Church, which opened in 1871. The houses were replaced by London County Council flats shortly after 1931 and the church was replaced by Stamford Hill Library after 1966.

Another rural Stamford Hill scene, this time from just north of the Portland Avenue junction, looking north. The horse tram belongs to the North Metropolitan Tramway Company, so this view dates from around 1903. Three of the mid-nineteenth-century houses hidden behind the trees on the right survive today.

These shops in Stamford Hill Broadway, on the corner with Clapton Common, were part of a development of around 1912. They replaced Cedar House and its grounds, which had dated from around 1760. This view is from the early 1920s; the tram is about to turn round the corner up Stamford Hill and along the short length of track in Egerton Road, behind the camera, to the depot in Rookwood Road. A. Stapleton, who had the shop next to the bank, ran a flourishing milk delivery and dairy business in the area for many years.

Another view of the Broadway, on what looks like a gloomy midwinter's day around 1910, with plenty of horse muck showing up on the cobblestones. The card was sent to a woman in Grimsby by Fred, who had cycled down from Lincolnshire in September 1911 and may have stopped at one of the Broadway shops to buy this card.

Continuing northward, this view of around 1914 was taken from the corner of Amhurst Park, looking north. The loaded carts are about to cross the tram tracks swinging into Egerton Road. The small building behind the signs was once the north lodge of the Craven Park estate, established in the early nineteenth century. The last owner was the philanthropist, Samuel Morley, and after his departure in 1870 the estate was gradually sold for building by Reuben Button. By 1914 the process was all but complete and Reuben's son, A.E. Button, has plastered up adverts for new buildings, including those on the north corner of Clapton Common and Stamford Hill. The main house, also Craven Lodge, was demolished in 1904; the little gate lodge lasted for another ten years after this view.

The garden of the Shrubbery, the first house in High Road, Tottenham, on the west side, just over the Hackney border. The card was sent by Mrs E.M. Harvey to her sister shortly after the Christmas rush had died down. For this Mrs Harvey was thankful, as she kept the post office at No. 188 Stamford Hill on the corner with Olinda Road, just across the road from home. The Shrubbery's narrow garden widened out and ran right down to the railway; this was later lost to an extension of Hillside Road. The photograph could date from around 1900, but the card was overprinted, perhaps on the death of Mr Harvey, around 1914.

Stamford Hill was also used to describe the southern part of Tottenham High Road, and this view shows that part of the road just to the north of the Hackney boundary, in around 1920. St Ignatius's Catholic Church had its origins in a Jesuit training college, established in 1894. This massive church, designed by Benedict Williams replaced the original church in 1903, serving the college and the Catholic parish.

A modified 'E' type tram stands by Cohen's smoked salmon shop at No. 170 Clapton Common on route No. 53. The 'E' types were subjected to various alterations, including the front windows on the lower deck. Although this view is undated, it must have been taken in 1938 or early 1939. Route No. 53 was one of the last to keep its trams, but the service finished on 5 March 1939, when trolleybus route No. 653 took over.

Alkham Road, from just north of the junction with Cazenove Road. These houses were opposite Clapton Hall and were built in 1878. The card was sent by a resident of one of the houses on the other side.

Bergholt Crescent from the Cranwich Road end, looking east. Bergholt Crescent was laid out around 1885 and building work started on the houses in the following year. This view was sent as a new year card in 1906.

Clapton Hall, on the east side of Alkham Road, was built in 1879 and may originally have been linked to a Congregational church, but it was run by the brethren by 1884. In that year they held four services on Sundays with additional meetings on Mondays and Fridays. In 1903, not long before this view was taken, 286 attended Sunday morning service and 324 Sunday afternoon service.

Cabs await passengers from the next train outside Stamford Hill station on Amhurst Park, c. 1910. It looks as if there has been a spot of bother with the drains and a workman is investigating. Stamford Hill station was built for the opening of the Enfield branch in 1872, and F. Warren & Co. had established its coal office by the mid-1880s.

Amhurst Parade, on the north side of Amhurst Park, looking west from near the junction with Stamford Hill, *c.* 1935. Only part of the Parade, dating from around 1910–12 is visible. Beyond the advert for the latest attraction at the Stamford Hill Super Cinema (opened at Nos. 152–8 Clapton Common in 1925) were the former Elm Bank and Henley Lodge, which had become a nursing institute by 1921. These were later to make way for the Yesodey Hatorah Grammar School, which was in operation by 1947.

Just over the Hackney border inside Stoke Newington was St Andrew's Church Hall, Bethune Road. It was built in 1904, north of the church and vicarage, and was only a year or so old when this view was taken. Both hall and vicarage were demolished for flats around 1982.

Boys pose obligingly outside Nos. 10–12 Chardmore Road, *c*. 1912. Running between Filey Avenue and Clapton Common, the road was constructed in 1889 and the houses were built in the next two to three years.

Cranwich Road from the Dunsmure Road end, *c*. 1922. George Mudge began as a carriage proprietor and had recently gone over to motors; within three years the carriages were to go altogether. Behind the horse and cart is the junction with Durley Road, with the rest of Cranwich Road bearing sharply off to the left. The houses in this view date from around 1886.

Darenth Road from the Portland Avenue junction, in a Burr's Library view, *c.* 1905. The road was laid out around 1883, with the bulk of the houses at this end of the road following in 1884. The two on the right date from four years later.

Denver Road lies just to the south of Bergholt Crescent and this view is looking east from the Cranwich Road junction towards Durley Road, probably around 1905. The middle house on the left is to let, a reminder that the bulk of the properties would have been rented and not owner-occupied at this time.

The spire of Stamford Hill Congregational Church rises above the end of Dunsmure Road in this view of around 1910, taken from near the junction with Glaserton Road. The houses on this side were built between 1885 and 1887. The card was sent by a resident of No. 20, which is in the block beyond the visible road junction with Wilderton Road.

Durley Road looking north from the corner with Cranwich Road towards Amhurst Park, c. 1904. The children have been sent out shopping, and they pause in the empty street. The creeper has had almost twenty years to become established, as houses on this side of the road date from 1886.

Another house is to let just beyond the horse and cart, this time in Durlston Road. If the man had moved his van, No. 57 would have been visible, which was the home of Henry Pinner, who sent the card in July 1922. He was not very well at the time – perhaps it was the ill effects of watching the whole place being cleaned round him, which he noted on the back of this card. The road was laid over the nursery land north of Northwold Road in 1894, and this view looks towards the sharp bend as the road turns east to meet Geldeston Road.

Perhaps Stamford Hill was regarded as a better address than Stoke Newington, or maybe the card maker was confused, but this photograph of Fairholt Road was taken from the junction with St Andrew's Road, looking east. Bethune Road is at the far end and this is just south of the East Reservoir in Stoke Newington, around 1905. The houses were the work of William Osment and date from 1883 to 1885.

Bends in the road lent a little variety to the street view. This is Forburg Road, looking north-east to the Clapton Common junction beyond the bend. The road dates from 1888 and the houses from a year or so later.

'I sent my sister for a picture postcard and she bought back this very uninteresting card,' complained the sender of this scene of Glasserton Road looking north in August 1915. However, she goes on to record a Zeppelin raid that had happened while she was away, causing considerable damage. Glasserton Road, dating from around 1892–3, escaped unscathed.

Linthorpe Road was laid out in 1885 between Stamford Hill and East Bank. This is the north side of the road, showing houses that were built between 1886 and 1889.

Grove Lane in the 1860s was a turning off Stamford Hill running due south of Grove Road and meeting the narrow lane called Birdcage Walk as it ran north towards what is now Oldhill Street. By the early 1890s Birdcage Walk north of the junction had become Oldhill Street and houses were in the course of construction. This view of around 1905 was taken from alongside the British Oak public house, looking west, with the turning for Kyverdale Road on the right. Grove Lane became Lampard Grove in 1939.

The southern part of Kyverdale Road was laid out in 1878, but this view of around 1905 shows what was originally Upper Kyverdale Road, beyond the junction with Grove Lane, looking north to where Lynmouth Road crosses and beyond to Portland Avenue. The houses here were built between 1882 and 1883, and the road was united under one name by 1897.

Northfield Road lies due north of Linthorpe Road and this view shows the west end of the road, with an ice cart heading east on a hot summer's day around 1904. The road was laid out in 1885 and the houses at this end of the road were built two years later.

Mr Brown the nurseryman is peering out of his greenhouse next to No. 45 Portland Avenue on an early spring day around 1920. The carts are going towards the London County Council depot at the junction of Portland Avenue and Darenth Road. This had started life as the horse tram depot for the North Metropolitan Tramways Company in 1873 and still has the company name on the brickwork. Tracks ran along Portland Avenue from Stamford Hill, through the depot to Clapton Common. It was acquired by the LCC when the company's lease expired in 1906 and then ceased to be used for trams. The houses date from 1905.

East Bank was laid out by the Tyssen surveyor, Chester Cheston in 1885, and, as the name implies, runs along the east side of the railway. The houses were built in the next three years. This view of around 1905, taken just south of the Northfield Road junction, also shows a schoolroom, built in the back garden of one of the houses in Amhurst Park around 1899. This seems to have been built for private use; by 1929 it was used by St Leonards College and by 1953 it was a synagogue.

This is West Bank, on the other side of the railway, also looking north on a spring day. The road was laid out in 1884 and the houses were built over the next three years.

This was someone's idea of a Valentine card, sent to Hampshire in 1908. No. 43 East Bank was on the corner of Dunsmure Road; the sender may well have been one of the Saxton family, who had recently moved in.

Walsingham Road runs between Rendlesham and Nightingale Roads and was constructed in 1863, with houses built over the following ten years. This rather empty view, showing the original railings to good effect, dates from around 1908.

The Agapemonite Church, on the Rookwood Road corner with Clapton Common and the adjoining Tower House, c. 1902. The winged beasts, representing the four evangelists, can just be seen on this extraordinary church, built for the followers of Henry James Prince in 1893–6 to the design of J. Morris. Prince died in 1899 and in 1902 the church witnessed the enthronement of his successor, John Hugh Smyth-Pigott, who proclaimed himself the Messiah and then had to face a hostile crowd. It is said that he claimed he could walk across Clapton pond, but there is no record of his making the attempt. The Agapemonites ceased to use the church in the 1920s and it was acquired by the Ancient Catholic Church in 1956.

Model yachts were a local passion and Clapton Common pond was a popular place to sail them, as this turn-of-the-century view shows. Hackney had its own model yacht club, a branch of the British Model Yacht Racing Association, and was active in the late 1920s.

Section Nine

UPPER CLAPTON

Clapton was once Clopton, 'the farm on the hill', possibly an Anglo-Saxon reference to a

former Roman villa that may once have stood at the edge of what is now Springfield Park.

The road through Clapton was originally Hackney Lane, and at its northern end it ran

through Broad Common, later Clapton Common. The division into Upper and Lower

Clapton came into common use at the end of the eighteenth century, the dividing line being

the Lea Bridge Road, which on its present alignment dates from 1745. This view of

around 1901 by Gordon Smith shows Clapton Common and St Thomas's Church,

originally a proprietary chapel of ease built by John Devall around 1774 for local tenants.

The row of houses to the north, dating from the 1790s, survives, but those to the south,

nearest to the camera, were demolished before 1959 for the Broad Common estate.

This is Champion House, No. 24 Clapton Common, and part of the row of houses called Champion Place, which were built on Tyssen estate land on the east side of the road shortly after 1825. In 1914 the house was occupied by Charles Stapleton, whose daughter Blanche sent the card as an invite to tea in 1912. The whole of Champion Place was one of the casualties of the postwar changes that swept through Upper Clapton, and it was cleared for the Fawcett estate in the mid-1950s.

A horse tram of the North Metropolitan Tramways waits at the terminus outside the Swan Hotel at the Common, in an Alfred Braddock view of around 1880. The tram route was extended from Lower Clapton in 1875 and was to be linked to Stamford Hill in 1902. The hotel proprietor seems to have modelled his bird on the design used by Bryant & May, the match manufacturers, though his public house, once the White Swan, dates from at least eighty years before that company began trading in 1861.

Opposite: the Salvation Army had early links with Hackney, through its founder, General William Booth, who lived on Mare Street from 1865 and moved to Clapton Common in 1880. Two years later the army's headquarters moved to the former London Orphan Asylum on Lower Clapton Road. Given this focus on Clapton, it is not suprising that the army took over other premises, among them No. 4 Clapton Common, which became their staff college around 1910. The house was part of Champion Place and had been home to one of Hackney's mayors, Francis Howse, in 1906. It was another casualty of the Fawcett estate development.

Another horse tram has paused for Alfred Braddock, by Cedar Lodge at the junction with Springfield, around 1903. The house that will shortly be the Salvation Army College is just visible through the trees next door. Cedar Lodge, named from some splendid cedars in its back garden, was the residence of Sir Walter Johnson, whose family auctioneering business was based at Hackney Road. Johnson was the second mayor of Hackney, and founder of a home for nurses in Clapton. He died here in 1912.

St Thomas's Church and the junction with Oldhill Street, *c.* 1904. On the left is Vincent Arthur's confectionery and post office. Oldhill Street began life as Hill Street shortly before 1774. St Thomas's Church acquired its own parish in 1828. Enlarged in the same year and substantially remodelled in 1873, the body of the church was destroyed in the Second World War and was rebuilt afterwards.

Stepping back on to the Common, this view shows some of the houses in Oldhill Street. The house next to the post office was the temporary home of the Stamford Hill synagogue in 1914, which was probably the Beth Hamedrash congregation that moved to Grove Lane in 1918.

Cazenove Road was created around 1867, and was originally Foulden Road. It was later extended to Stamford Hill and its original southern part became Fountayne Road. This view from the early 1920s is looking east towards the Fountayne Road junction.

Cazenove Road again, from the Fountayne Road junction. The houses date from around 1878. The road took its name from an early nineteenth-century family, who owned a large house on the east side of Upper Clapton Road, which was demolished around 1894, prior to the construction of Moresby Road.

Upper Clapton Road, looking north from the corner with Northwold Road, *c.* 1914. The boy with his bike is outside Toop's the butchers and beyond is George Charlton & Son's fruit shop. In the middle distance is Upper Clapton Congregational Church, which could trace the history of its congregation back to 1812. This building was built in 1851–2 and seated a thousand people. After bomb damage in 1944, it was rebuilt in 1956.

Welford's dairy shop and yard at No. 83 Upper Clapton Road lay almost next door to the Congregational church. Welford's had taken over the business of James Rumball & Son around 1910, when this view was taken. Rumball's had been established a few doors down the road in the early 1870s. The Welford family had their own cowsheds in London at the end of the nineteenth century and also kept cows at Spring Hill Farm, delivering milk three times per day to customers. The firm was taken over by United Dairies around 1928.

Looking south along Upper Clapton Road around 1914, this view includes the Crooked Billet, which in this form dates from its rebuilding as a tea garden and covered bowling alley after 1840. The present public house dates from the early 1950s, and all the other buildings in this view north of the railway station, just visible in the distance, have been cleared away.

Clapton station is advertising excursions to Clacton in this view of around 1910, with the new electric trams dating from the year before standing alongside. Electricity is also in evidence in the lights; these were put up by Hackney Borough Council after 1901, powered by its new generating station on Millfields Road.

The splendid garden of Walter Robinson and his daughter lay on the north side of Holmbury View. Originally the grounds had formed part of Springfield Cottage, but prior to the demolition in 1908 this part of the land, which was on a steep slope down to the River Lea, was acquired by Robinson, who lived opposite at No. 1 Holmbury View. Taking advantage of the slope, the family created a terrace garden, seen at its best in early summer. This view shows part of the terraces in the summer of 1908. The following year the garden was given up for building, and after a long period as a rubbish tip became the site of Springfield Park paddling pool and pavilion.

This is Ryde House, at No. 138 Upper Clapton Road, on the corner with Mount Pleasant Road, around 1905. For some years it had been a doctor's surgery, shared between Herbert Powell and John Gundlach, and it was Mrs Gundlach who sent this card to a friend in 1906. The house was substantially altered in 1934, but its core may have survived until 1960.

Springfield was originally Spring Place, and the row of houses on the south side probably date from the 1820s. By the time Martin Sander took this view around 1910, the land on the left had been saved from the developers and had become Springfield Park, which opened in 1905. Even after the First World War Springfield was still a good address, and one of those who moved here was George Butters, whose father had been one of the builders of South Hackney sixty years before. The houses were all demolished for the Lea View estate in 1938.

Section Ten

SPRINGFIELD AND THE RIVER LEA

It was in the grounds of what is now Springfield Park that Roman remains were found in the 1820s, including a stone coffin. At the bottom of Spring Hill there was a tile kiln works in the early nineteenth century with its own dock from the Lea, since filled in. Later a small settlement grew up between Bakers Hill and Big Hill on the slopes up from the Lea. The park was not created without a fight, and supporters included Thomas Garland, who sold his own house, Spring Hill House, in 1904 so that its estate could be added to the new park. Another house, the Chesnuts, was also demolished, but Springfield House, seen in this view and dating from the 1820s, survived.

Nanny is helping with the children near the lake in Springfield Park, one summer just before the First World War. The grounds of Springfield House had a lake, which altered in size over the years. It was enlarged after the park was created and an island was included in the design. The elaborate flower-beds show the municipal care that had been lavished on the park.

Springfield Park formed part of one child's happy holiday with her aunt in 1930, and she may have enjoyed the paddle-boats on Springfield Park's lake.

The ideal place for a skip, another view of the park around 1912.

RIVER LEA. SPRING HILL

At the bottom of Spring Hill is High Bridge, a footbridge leading on to Walthamstow Marshes. This view of around 1905 was taken from the Walthamstow side and looks back to Spring Hill. High Bridge dates from the late eighteenth century; prior to that a ferry crossed the Lea here. There were many rowing clubs here, as well as boats for hire on both sides of the river, and one of the hire places is visible to the right of the bridge. On the left is River Villa, by this date a social club, and behind it Solomons Cottage and some of the buildings belonging to Spring Hill Farm. All of these were soon to vanish with the creation of Springfield Park.

A cold day for boating, as a crew prepares to pull away from Jacob Tyrell's boatyard, *c*. 1905. By 1914 there were thirteen rowing clubs based here, including the Tressillian Ladies Rowing Club, a breach of a previously all-male bastion.

It looks as if all the staff and customers have emptied out of the Bee Hive public house to pose along with the Robin Hood ferryman in this view of around 1904. The Robin Hood public house can be seen on the far right, above the waterside houses. The Bee Hive stood alongside a small turning for Retreat Cottages and was one of three pubs serving the tiny settlement bounded by Mount Pleasant Lane, Bakers Hill and Big Hill, together with its summer visitors, who came for the rural scenes as well as the beer.

Opposite: although a large number of Hackney's factories were along the Lea or in the Hackney Wick area, there were many exceptions. This was the works of the Carbonic Acid Gas Company at No. 142 Lea Bridge Road, around 1914, which was established here in 1890. An adjoining row of houses, Otley Terrace, which presented windowless walls to the street, were high on Hackney Borough Council's slum clearance list in the early 1930s.

A view from the other side of the Lea, showing all three pubs. To the north, beyond the last row of cottages (Elizabeth Place), are the buildings of the Triton Chemical Works, already established by the mid-1880s. The Bee Hive originally resembled its neighbour, the Anchor and Hope beer house (the white building closer to the camera), but it was rebuilt in 1902. The houses fronting the Lea were always susceptible to flooding and this provided the incentive for Hackney Borough Council to clear the area and replace the older housing with flats in 1939. The Bee Hive survives, but unlike the other two pubs, it lost its licence.

A brief return to Spring Hill before we leave this part of Hackney. This view is looking down the hill from what will become the park lodge in around 1903. The cricket pavilion and tennis courts belonged to the Upper Clapton Cricket and Lawn Tennis Club, and were also used by three other tennis clubs in 1901. The land opposite the lodge was taken for the building of Lingwood Road in 1908.

Further up the hill, one of Welford's dairy carts pauses for a cyclist. This group of houses, just south of the Overlea Road junction, was built shortly after 1908.

Section Eleven

THE TRADESMEN

The staff of this branch of the Maypole Dairy Company at No. 142 Stoke Newington High Street are in the first view of a small selection of shops and businesses that chose to use the postcard as a form of publicity. The photographer commissioned by the dairy company to go round all of their branches on 1 May 1914, caught a typically crowded shop window, as well as activity next door as Samuel Joel busies himself arranging rhubarb and spring onions. The Maypole Dairy was to expand further and by the end of the 1920s had shops in Kingsland High Street and Mare Street. This one lasted until the mid-1930s.

ANOTHER EXPEDITION TO THE POLE
Always at your Service!
CHAS. PETERS,
30, ALLEN ROAD, STOKE NEWINGTON, N.

Artistic licence has enlarged Charles Peter's shop at No. 30 Allen Road, around 1906. The shop was one of a row in this Albert Town road dating from the 1850s, which was named after the Quaker William Allen, a Paradise Row resident. Polar expeditions were very much in the news at the time, prompting the pun. The red and white barber's pole recalled the old guild link between barbers and surgeons, though Bill Manley recalled shaving cuts being treated not with plaster, but with the rapid application of a cigarette paper!

W.R. Tebbs's hairdressing saloon at No. 154 Green Lanes as it appeared in 1912. Mr Tebbs had served five years with Mr Pitts at Highbury Corner before he took on the Green Lanes business from another hairdresser in the row of shops just south of the Church Street junction. Trade was good as he was in business until 1928. Unlike most proud shop proprietors, he seemed unwilling to be included in the photograph of his shop.

John Wesley Lott's bakery at No. 33 Nevill Road had just installed new electric ovens when this view was taken in 1929. The firm's handcart stands alongside in Osterley Road and it looks as if son and grandson have been included in the postcard. After many years as a bakery the shop is now a private house again. On the opposite corner is the Nevill Arms, where a German bomb landed in 1915, narrowly missing the landlady, Laura Kirkby. The advert on the side of the building, 'To What Red Hell', is for an early talking picture adaption of a stage play starring Sybil Thorndike and John Hamilton, which was the current attraction at the Electric Coliseum on Stoke Newington Road.

'Madam', proclaimed this early example of junk mail, 'We desire to announce that the latest novelties and fashion styles are now on view at T.H. Hinton's establishment, soliciting the favour of an early visit. . . .' Hinton's drapery business stood at Nos. 132–6 Upper Clapton Road in a row built around 1895. Hinton's was established by 1900, though this view may date from around 1905 when it had expanded into all three shops, but No. 132 had been given up by 1914 and the business does not seem to have survived the First World War.

George Mudge has already featured in another Cranwich Road view; this is his own card, issued shortly before 1914. His recently acquired motors mark the change over from the horse-drawn job-master work that had previously formed the bulk of his business. The proud owner stands in front of the nearest car and his family peer from the doorstep.

Noah Crisp stands outside his newsagent's shop at No. 96 Boleyn Road on 7 January 1907. It looks as if he has had a new shop-front installed. The camera has come close enough to pick up all the poster headlines, including the new merger of the tube railway companies and the latest series of Hornsey Library lectures. Also the latest from the *Daily Express*, which seems to have followed a consistently sensational line on London local government over the years.

Jack Frank Ewen and his son stand proudly outside their house, No. 83 Windus Road, with the range of carts used in the family business of carpet cleaning and chimney sweeping, in around 1912. Jack added vacuum cleaners to his stock-in-trade after the First World War. By 1923 Arthur Ewen was trading as a chimney sweep only from this address and the business had ceased altogether by 1925.

Churches clearly came to Coates for their printing jobs, as his window advertises work for St Matthias's Church and the Rectory Road Men's Own in this view of the ground floor of No. 5 Howard Road, *c.* 1905. Alfred P. Coates had set himself up here before 1885 and by this time was sharing the work with Harry Coates. However, the business was to last less than ten more years, and was a grocery shop by 1914.

Charles Skinner has made sure that the entrance to his yard alongside his house, No. 47 Grayling Road, near the Bouverie Road end of the street in 1904 proclaims his trade. His painting and decorating business had been established in a former stable yard in the early 1890s. The house next door was home to the Manor Park Club from 1884 to the end of the nineteenth century, but by 1901 was used by Albert Pease in his church organ building work.

SCHOOLS, PRIVATE
AND PUBLIC

Wordsworth Road School on Friday 22 June 1923, when local schools all had a day of

glorious weather for the third annual Stoke Newington School Sports, held in Finsbury

Park. Wordsworth Girls came fifth out of eight schools, with only nine points, for running,

skipping, long-jump, high-jump and the egg-and-spoon race. The boys did better, coming

top with thirty-nine points. Wordsworth Road School, opened in 1878 by Hornsey School

Board, closed in 1956. After two years as a temporary school for Clissold Park School, the

buildings were demolished for the Horizon Special School.

Paradise House School, seen in this Charles Martin view of around 1905, had been founded in Lordship Park in 1876, but moved to its Paradise Row location three years later. It was a boys' day and boarding school and pupils were given education to matriculation (the equivalent of GCSE), with two large playgrounds, plunge baths for boarders and visits to Hornsey Road Baths in summer months. The pupils seem more interested in the school yard than the girls who have just passed, heading for the shops on Green Lanes.

Most of the houses in Springfield remained in private use, but No. 10 was an exception and around 1902 it became a children's home called The Nest, which was run by the Salvation Army. Although early directory entries do not make it clear, it was for girls only. Its ample garden provided plenty of space for outside activity, as the composite card and view of hoops and swings make clear. Springfield was close to the army's headquarters and the Mothers' Hospital, which were both in Lower Clapton Road.

This view of life at The Nest – showing the prams and the well-clothed children – would have emphasized the care the Salvation Army gave to the children entrusted to it, and would have been intended to help with fund-raising.

Another view of the children at The Nest with the wide range of toys that were available. The Nest survived into the 1930s, when the house, like its neighbours, was cleared for the construction of Lea View House. Somewhere there must be children who remember life there. Were they as well cared for as this view suggests?

The Sixth (Stoke Newington) Company of Girl Guides makes a happy group. The man in the middle may well be the minister of Devonshire Square Chapel, to which the Sixth Company was attached. Formed on 28 July 1916, six years after the Girl Guides were established nationally, the first captain was Miss Dodd, later Mrs Mackay, who may well be in this view. Although the postcard is undated, this view may date from the time the Guides received their royal charter, in 1922. The company was disbanded in May 1980.

We have already encountered Tower House at Clapton Common; this view of the house in service as a branch of Clarkes College dates from around 1910 and was sent by a teacher at the college to a friend. Clarkes College moved to Nos. 147–9 Stamford Hill and remained in business until 1962. Tower House had been replaced by Rookwood Court in 1935–6.

All the pupils and staff of Skinners School have gathered outside for a group photograph, in around 1905. The school was founded by the Skinners Company in 1890, following foundations for boys created at Tunbridge Wells and Tonbridge in Kent. This building was purpose built at Nos. 111 and 113 Stamford Hill for 250 girls, aged seven to eight at admission. The school was voluntary aided from 1949. After 1972 younger girls moved to the former Mount Pleasant School, but the school continues to serve Hackney pupils today.

The Willows in Paradise Row, which was built by banker George William Alexander in the late 1860s on the site of the westernmost house in the row, where he had lived since the late 1840s. Alexander passed the house over to the Mildmay Deaconess Institute in 1885 and it became a training centre, where young women of good education spent two years before working in missions all over London and abroad; it was just one part of a wider movement. The enlarged Willows, with its four reception rooms and twenty-three bedrooms was ideal for college use. This view from Paradise Row dates from 1929, when it had been renamed Kennaway Hall, after another change of ownership.

A game of netball is in progress at Kennaway Hall in the winter of 1926. The Willows estate was sold on Alexander's death in 1891 and the institution was able to acquire the freehold when the rest of the estate was sold for development. In 1918 The Willows was sold again, this time to the Church Missionary Society, which was already sending pupils there. Its president of thirty years standing, Sir John Kennaway, had died in the previous year, and the hall was renamed in his memory.

Trainees and staff pose for a group picture at Kennaway Hall in June 1921. The principal, Constance Mary Richardson, had just taken over, and was to stay for another seven years. Kennaway Hall and its two neighbouring houses were demolished for the construction of two blocks of London County Council flats, Taverner and Garland Houses, around 1953.

Springfield Girls' School at No. 56 Clapton Common was one of twenty-nine private schools in Hackney in 1906, when it was kept by Miss Henrietta Maria Richards. This view may date from her time, or from that of her successor, Miss A.F. Elliot, who was in charge from 1914 until the school closed in 1918. By that time only fifteen private schools remained, declining further so that by 1939 there were only three, and Hackney's long tradition of private schools stretching back to Pepys's time was coming to a close.

The Clapton School of Art, at No. 81 Clapton Common, was said to have the oldest house on the Common by one of its teachers, Florence Bagust, who sent this card to James Rennie of Mount Pleasant Lane in 1911. The house, dating from the later eighteenth century, had been the base for Mr Bryon's coaches in the early nineteenth century. After a period as a boarding school it was taken over by Alice Nyssen, the first head teacher of the art school, which had started in 1888 at No. 37. Florence Bagust was also a keen antiquarian and kept a series of scrapbooks and notes on the history of the Clapton area. Her postcard note mutters darkly about 'being very guarded about a Roman well', not, however, a Hackney one!

Girls drawing in the art school in 1916. Alice Nyssen was soon succeeded by the energetic Edith Giles, who kept up a high standard. However, the school was felt to be too small for the London County Council, which withdrew the grant in 1915. Florence, who had learnt to use a camera to good effect, recorded the last days of the school before its closure on 16 June 1916. In the late 1920s the house was used by St Thomas's Church. No. 81 and its neighbours were all casualties swept away for the construction of the Summit House estate in the mid-1950s.

Miss James kept the Northfield School for Girls, which she began at No. 109 Stamford Hill in 1884. By the late 1890s it had become the North Hackney High School for Girls, and had its own registered kindergarten, training college, school of housewifery and training college for domestic science. By then it had spread to three of the houses between Linthorpe and Northfield Roads. Miss Goodman had taken over from the long-serving Miss James by 1921 and the school continued until shortly after 1934, when it was acquired by the Jewish Secondary Schools Movement. Jewish girls were taught there until the Second World War. This view of an open-air class is from around 1905, in Miss James's time, and was sent as a Christmas card.

By contrast, this card of around 1905 shows a school board class with boys and girls more or less carefully divided. There is no location, though the fact that the photographer was based in Green Lanes suggests it is a Stoke Newington school.

The sewing class in progress at The Nest, Springfield, 1905.

Acknowledgements

The text on which this book is based was produced by Bill Manley, in turn based on the postcard collection of Dick Whetstone. The original book, complete at Bill Manley's death in January 1993, included only part of the N16 postal district, and, although intended to be a Stoke Newington book, left out those areas of the former borough west of Green Lanes. The book was also intended to have a single picture per page. In adapting it for publication, the geographical range was extended to take in Brownswood, and Upper Clapton and Stamford Hill were added to the Hackney part of Bill's original text, which had confined itself to the streets round Stoke Newington Common. To achieve this, some pictures were added from the visual collection of Hackney Archives Department and the publisher is grateful for the cooperation of the London Borough of Hackney. Special thanks are due to Dick Whetstone, for allowing the project to go ahead after Bill's death, and for the use of his extensive postcard collection again to extend the book.

Bill Manley drew on his own personal knowledge, together with help from several collections and a number of local people. On his behalf, I would like to thank the following:

The Alliance Club, Newington Green
David Webb of the Bishopsgate Institute Library
Rosemary Keen of the Church Missionary Society
John Field of the Clissold Park Users Group
Mrs A. Thwaites of the Girl Guides
Mr N. Bowdidge of the Great Eastern Railway Society
Sue McKenzie, formerly of Hackney Archives Department
Marilyn Gibson, Martin Tupper, Yasmeen Webb and Steve Smith of the Central Reference Library, London Borough of Islington
Len Phillips and Sid Holyland of the Islington Visitors Centre
Carl Malyon of J.D. Wetherspoon
John Rodwell, Roy Still and Keith W. Fern of the London Fire Brigade Museum
Jonathan Riddell of London Transport Museum
Dick Westrup of the Mildmay Club
Revd Allan Scott of St Mary's Church, Stoke Newington
Andrew Ward of Stoke Newington Library, London Borough of Hackney
Central Reference Library, City of Westminster

Bill added a personal debt, as ever, to Brenda Burkill and Marjie Manley.

In preparing Bill's original book for publication, I have carried out substantial additional research and added building dates for houses in the pictures where possible and relevant. I have drawn extensively on the *Victoria County History of Middlesex* articles on Stoke Newington and on Hackney (the latter in an advance draft copy). I am grateful to the County Editor, T.F.T. Baker, for access to this draft copy. The resulting work added to Bill's original text, and I have edited it to ensure a reasonable continuity of style throughout, but I hope that Bill's intentions, if not always his exact words, remain. Bill Manley was a regular user of Hackney Archives Department, and it had been our hope to have produced a history of entertainment in Hackney to match his work on Islington. Funding problems precluded this and I am pleased to have had this opportunity to ensure that his last project has come to fruition. I hope that he would have been pleased with the result.

David Mander
August 1995

A composite of Stoke Newington scenes of the 1920s, published by C. Degan, showing (clockwise): Clissold House, Church Street, Clissold Park and old St Mary's Church, with the new church in the centre. This example was posted in 1930.

Index